Navigating Important Events Without Appearing Clueless

NAVIGATING IMPORTANT EVENTS
WITHOUT APPEARING CLUELESS

Common sense advice, historical reflection, and gift-giving savvy

A Socially Savvy Book for all Ages

By Rebecca Black

CELESTIAL ARC PUBLISHING

CELESTIAL ARC PUBLISHING
ISBN-13: 9781081192655

DEDICATION

To my dearest friend and loving husband Walker Black. You have been my most ardent supporter and the very best editor a writer can have.

In memory of my daughter, Shannon. Thank you for your thoughtful edits and all our shared moments.

CONTENTS

INTRODUCTION

"Friends and good manners will carry you where money won't go." Margaret Walker

As I was perusing the newspaper recently, I came across a few distressing stories. In one, the happy couple returned a wedding shower gift for cash because they considered it less than perfect. They sent a check with a letter informing the astonished gift-givers not to attend the wedding. Another story was equally disturbing. In announcing the birth of her new child, the new mother sent flyers asking for cash to set up a college fund.

If those examples were not enough to demonstrate a lack of consideration, read on.

Imagine a baby shower held without the expectant mother, who was ill. Her guests not only held the event but also opened all her gifts in her absence.

Even more heartbreaking is the story of an expectant mother who suffered a miscarriage, only to have her mother-in-law take all the gifts she received and pass them on to another daughter who was expecting. One must wonder how people rationalize such thoughtless and hurtful actions.

In this book, we undertake an exploration of our social customs, focusing principally on the traditions surrounding gift-giving, grief-sharing, and celebrations. These practices originated in a past when life was structured very differently. Today, we often take these established traditions to a bizarre new level, pushing them past the limits of common courtesy. The belief that it is acceptable to open someone's gifts because they are ill, or to confiscate those gifts for another recipient, is a profound example of this modern aberration.

As we examine the evolution of these customs, I invite you to consider your own values and critically question your assumptions about these long-held traditions. Let us collectively re-examine the purpose of these rites and, perhaps, "Stop the madness!"

Something Special

I've included something you might not expect in a book such as this—thought bubbles. You'll recognize them by the: *. I hope you enjoy reading my, at times silly, thoughts.

Cheers!

WEDDINGS

A LITTLE HISTORY

The music at a wedding procession always reminds me of the music of soldiers going into battle. Heinrich Heine (1797-1856)

In Europe, a wedding during the Middle Ages was a family and community affair. When the couple decided to be together, they announced their intentions to the township, and the two were considered a wedded couple.

During the 15th century, the Council of Trent decreed that a formal wedding ceremony must be conducted by a priest, establishing the tradition of church weddings officiated by clergy. To encourage greater attendance at mass, priests often followed the ceremony with a religious service. Brides of that time wore garments resembling the wedding dresses seen today.

In contrast, during the early Saxon era, marriage by capture was common. The groom, accompanied by loyal tribesmen, would ride into a neighboring village to seize his bride, while his companions fended off her family. Traditionally, the groom held his bride in his left arm and his sword in his right, a detail many believe explains why brides stand to the left of the groom during modern ceremonies.

A woman from the groom's village would prepare the bride for the ceremony, making the bridal wreath, decorating for a bridal feast, and dressing her. The groom would then conceal his bride for a month—traditionally referred to as "a moon"—while drinking honey and mead, a sweet, fermented beverage. Hence, the honeymoon was born.

The tribesmen who aided in the capture are now our ushers and best man. Additionally, the woman who prepared the bride is now the maid of honor. These are our modern bridal party, and today they are close friends of both the bride and the groom.

The bachelor party actually began as an ancient Spartan custom. Close friends of the groom would come to a dinner provided by the groom on the eve of his wedding. His friends would offer their support.

In many cultures, marriages were—and in some cases still are—arranged by families. Dowries were traditionally paid to the groom or his family, both as compensation for supporting a household and as recognition of the perceived value of a son. In fact, throughout history, most cultures have incorporated some form of dowry into their marriage customs.

NOTE

The Anglo-Saxon word "Wed" referred to a contract between two families, which often occurred when the daughter was still an infant. The wedding is the ceremony where the couple is married.

Today's Weddings

Don't be a slave to someone else's idea of what you should do.
Live up to your values

Now that we have a little of the history of weddings, let us reflect upon what it has become.

In this country, women are thankfully no longer property— they cannot be stolen, bartered, or contracted at birth. Despite this progress, weddings have, in general, become a bloated production, much like a poorly scripted reality show. Media and merchant advertisers have clearly influenced this, popularizing ads that claim: "Your wedding is the most important day in your life."

This may be true, but just because the day is important for the couple does not mean that the bride should put her family and friends through an emotional roller coaster and financial ruin because she wants to play princess for a day.

Shouldn't the focus be on the fact that two people have found love and want to formalize and legalize their commitment? Love—not elaborate outfits or an avalanche of gifts—should be at the heart of the celebration.

Most women dream of walking down an aisle, dressed in a beautiful gown, with everyone around smiling. This is the perfect wedding; *everything is perfect.*

Now for the reality check. Nothing is perfect. Moreover, when we put that kind of pressure on ourselves and those around us, this *perfect* wedding could fall apart, hurting all involved. The result could be a perfect-looking wedding, but it may cost you the price of a down payment on a house, the equivalent of five years of investing, or perhaps your relationships with family members.

An example comes to mind. My friend's son is marrying a normally rational woman who has succumbed to the diva syndrome. She became so demanding that the family started to call her the princess. How unfortunate that she is not yet part of the family, but has already alienated herself.

Am I proposing abandoning the dream wedding and discarding traditions we cherish? Not in the least. I humbly suggest rational thought and common sense. And remember to enjoy the happy day. Live a little and lighten up. Accept that none of us can – or should – demand everyone to do exactly as we command.

Furthermore, consider this. What is most important: the *person* you are marrying, or the value of the wedding and gifts received?

Reflecting on the brief history lesson presented at the beginning of this chapter, and considering what modern weddings have become, it becomes clear that our traditions are shaped by time and circumstance. At some point, someone decided what elements should be included in the union of two people. This realization suggests that we, too, hold the power to create our own wedding traditions.

WEDDING GIFTS

Let's consider the rationale behind wedding gift-giving. People give gifts because they care about the couple. Even if the presents do not meet expectations, it's important to remember that loved ones are under no obligation to buy anything. Gifts are given as genuine acts of kindness.

As with many other wedding traditions, someone, at some point in history, decided that giving gifts to newlyweds was a wonderful idea. Most of us enjoy receiving gifts, but it's essential to remain grateful. Consequently, we should also remember to write and send thank-you notes promptly.

Treat others kindly and as you wish to be treated.

WEDDING QUESTION

Question

Dear Rebecca,

My fiancée and I are having a destination wedding in Puerto Rico and expecting about 120 guests. We are currently living in Italy, but will be moving back to the States shortly before the wedding. Given that we cannot provide a shipping address yet and will be traveling by air (making it impossible to transport gifts), how should we clearly and politely inform guests on our invitations that we cannot accept physical gifts? Thanking you in advance.

Respectfully,

A Confused Groom

Reply:

Dear Confused Groom,

Using old-fashioned wedding etiquette, you wouldn't inform guests about gift preferences on the invitation, as if you assume guests want to give you a gift.

Nevertheless, they do. Therefore, the best way to get the information out is by 'word of mouth.' Make sure that everyone close to you knows your preferences. Or you could include a card inside the invitation envelope. Example: As we will be flying to and from Puerto Rico and moving homes shortly after, we are unable to accommodate physical gifts or large items. You could also create a wedding website with one page (not the first page) devoted to your gift dilemma.

Another option is to choose the address of a family member in the U.S. as the RSVP return address for your guests. Your guests will then have an address where they may send their gifts. This person may want to help you keep track of the guests and gifts anyway.

Many people feel closer to the happy couple when they offer assistance. I know I always like to pour the Champagne—perhaps because I love it!

Congratulations on your upcoming wedding!

Warm regards,

Rebecca

BRIDAL SHOWERS

A History Lesson

Most sources agree that the tradition of bridal showers began in Holland, where a young Dutch girl fell in love with a poor miller.

The reason for the miller's lack of wealth was that he shared much of his belongings with the community, thus endearing him to all in town.

Her father withheld her dowry when they married, so the community responded by *showering* the bride with the necessities needed to set up a home.

Over time, this type of kindness and sharing became a wedding tradition, which eventually led to the end of the dowry system.

Bridal showers became common in the late nineteenth century, centering on strengthening friendships, providing moral support, and planning for marriage.

TODAY'S SHOWERS

Today's showers tend to focus on gifts, multiple showers, and couples' parties. Given that many couples live together for some time before marriage, with both working and earning income, it's easy to wonder what purpose the shower serves today. Hmm... Are we putting too much pressure on our friends and family? This is double-gift dipping after all.

Every situation is different, and every couple is different. Perhaps some people need extra help. Nevertheless, we should look at this tradition a little closer. Celebrating the fact that two people find each other is positive, so *people* should be our focus, not *things*.

BRIDAL SHOWER ETIQUETTE

One redeeming feature of the modern bridal shower is that the secondary purpose is to help guests feel as if they are a part of the wedding-planning process. This is the primary reason why only those invited to the wedding are invited to the wedding shower.

Another *rule* is that the family shouldn't host the bridal shower. Some do because of local customs, but it is best to avoid doing so if possible. The reason is simple. The shower is a gift-giving event, and the family will often try to garner as many gifts as possible for family members. It is only human nature. Therefore, it is viewed as self-serving for the family to host.

One of the more negative aspects of family members hosting the bridal shower is when they host the mega-shower. A phenomenon popular with the mother of the bride as the host. Usually, she invites a copious number of guests, on par with a wedding reception. Of course, some brides request these through their bridesmaids as well. *Yikes!* Nevertheless, mothers have been responsible for hosting these ill-conceived events of late.

Bridal showers are traditionally small, intimate gatherings designed to make guests feel involved in the wedding planning process. Yet with the rise of the mega-shower, hosts now invite anywhere from 40 to 150 guests—sometimes including everyone on the wedding guest list.

Guests often view this as greedy. Not one guest wrote to me praising the host for a wonderful party. Conversely, every single guest who wrote to me complained about the double-gift-grabbing vibe they felt about the event. I must agree.

Bridal Shower Question

Question

My daughter is planning a wedding for September. She has been living with her boyfriend since December. In truth, they don't need anything for their apartment. I want to host a shower for her and would like to know if it is proper. I wish to have brunch at a restaurant by selling tickets. The money left over after paying for the meals is her gift.

Second dilemma, her father and I are paying for the wedding. Do we have to list the groom's parents on the wedding invitations? I am creating the invitations on the computer, and they will just about hold the info needed.

I've received several comments about this already, from his side. His parents feel that they must be listed on the invitations. Any advice you could give would be greatly appreciated.
Thank you.

Reply:

Dear Is It Proper,

Yikes! No, and please no. Please do not host your daughter's bridal shower. Mothers should not host their daughter's shower, as it could appear greedy and as begging for gifts. Moreover, expecting gifts is more of the same. All gift giving should be optional and never expected.

In addition, selling tickets is not polite. That is like telling her friends and family to pay for her party and give her money just because she has decided to get married. If you invite, you pay. Guests never pay for a party they were invited to attend.

His parents do not need to be included on the invitation. They may be included, but it is not necessary. If they are contributing to any of the expenses, including them is a nice gesture.

If this is a formal wedding, the invitations should be engraved or printed by a professional stationer. Other than that, the computer-generated invitations should be fine. However, please do not computer-generate the labels for the envelopes, thank-you notes, or letters. These should be handwritten.

Finally, since parents are no longer financially responsible for their children's weddings, they also no longer plan. The couple should make all the decisions, including how the invitations appear.

Sincerely,

Rebecca

BABY SHOWERS

BABY SHOWER HISTORY

"Yesterday is a memory, tomorrow is a mystery and today is a gift."

Ancient cultures, such as the Egyptians and Romans, gave handmade gifts to newborns or to the parents in celebration of the birth. However, the history of the modern baby shower is more recent. In fact, it began after WWII.

Men returned from war and wanted to start families, which became *the baby boom.* New parents needed moral support and the family wanted to share in the excitement of the newest addition. Many of these families started with very little. After all, the men had been fighting in a war not building a nest egg.

TODAY'S BABY SHOWER

When a new mother brings that little bundle home, it is a wonderful and exciting time. At the same time, it can be a stressful and confusing time. New mothers tend to doubt their competence and the baby's needs are all consuming. Friends and family, this is an excellent time to jump in with both feet. Perhaps Emily Post was correct to suggest that the baby shower would be best hosted after the child is born.

There's no rule about when the shower can be held.

As is the case with all traditions, we should evaluate for ourselves if this is a tradition we believe in. Do we wish to participate? Truly, we can and should decide for ourselves.

Nevertheless, if this is the mother's first child, we should be there for support at the very least. Additionally, please don't forget adoptive mothers. These moms need as much support as any other mother.

THE ETIQUETTE INVOLVED

For the baby shower, please do not request gifts or money. Nevertheless, a gift registry is helpful and can be included in the invitation.

Guests are not obligated, however, to give a gift even though they received an invitation. All gift giving is optional. We just assume that a shower is a gift-giving event and a little guidance via a registry is helpful.

FUNERALS AND GRIEVING

A History Lesson

When anthropologists discover an ancient site where a civilization or a community lived, they typically search for evidence of burial ceremonies. This evidence reveals volumes about how the community cared for each other and how they lived. It also tells them that they are studying intelligent beings.

Cultures develop these traditions out of respect for the dead and the families who grieve.

Most are familiar with the ancient Egyptian burials. The most interesting aspect, of course, was their practice of mummification; this was done so the spirit would have a body in the next world. Egyptians also believed the dead would need useful, everyday-type items for the next world, so these items were buried with the body. This demonstrates their care and respect for the dead. Egyptians would save during their entire lives for their burial procedure; it was expensive and an important part of their belief system.

Why is it important to study the Egyptian burial traditions or more current traditions of grieving? I believe that most of us want to express our respect for those *who have passed* and those *who are left behind* to grieve.

To do this, we should learn – at the very least – some traditions before we can understand this process and subsequently, we can then properly show our support for our grieving friend and for those who have departed.

JEWISH TRADITIONS

Jewish burial traditions sprang from Genesis; Abraham, grief stricken, sought a suitable burial site for his beloved wife, Sarah. Based on the same story is the Jewish grieving period, which is very structured and designed to respect the dead, give the mourner direction and ease her back into a normal life.

If you wish to comfort a Jewish friend during her trying time, there are a few etiquette rules to follow.

THE ETIQUETTE INVOLVED

Probably the most difficult tradition for the non-Jew is to withhold comfort from your grieving friend before and directly after the funeral. Only *very* close friends and relatives visit during this time. Traditionally, the mourner directs all attention to the departed. Your friend will only visit you after the Shiva, the seven days of mourning. However, you may visit her during that period, but expect and exercise silence.

There is no viewing of the body; this is interpreted as an insult to the dead. Noise, of any kind, is also insulting. So, no talking, laughing, or even eulogizing at the burial. However, in some cases, a rabbi or close friend may offer a eulogy.

Expect your friend to tear or cut her clothing, although the more recent custom is to pin a piece of torn material to her blouse to symbolize this first formal act of mourning. She must do this alone without comfort.

She may or may not participate in shoveling dirt on the casket. It is an old custom revisited. It demonstrates concern for the departed and is offered to help the dead on their journey. You are not required to stay.

Flowers are not part of the Jewish tradition—donations to the deceased's favorite charity are a good choice.

Upon your visit to your friend's home, the door will not be locked, so please do not knock; there should be silence. Before entering, it is customary to rinse your hands. If unsure what to do, look around for a bowl to use.

Perhaps your friend doesn't follow this custom, or perhaps this family would prefer visitors to wash their hands in the house. Commonly, we tend to follow some traditions and ignore others. So, quietly watch what others are doing.

Once inside, avoid speaking; the mourner should be the first to speak. She will be sitting on a short stool or box to symbolize a humbled state. So, do not expect her to greet you; she will not socialize. The pious do not greet or respond for the first three days of the Shiva. They also do not engage in any entertainment for the full seven.

She is expected to remain in the home for seven days and will avoid makeup or any signs of vanity. This may be difficult, as a friend, to watch your friend looking haggard and in deep sorrow, but this is her traditional form of grieving.

"Say not in grief 'he is no more' but live in thankfulness that he was" Hebrew
proverb

The mourner does not cook or provide any refreshments for visitors; this is not a wake.

As a display of support, family or neighbors bring food in directly after the burial, to begin the Shiva. The food is usually round, symbolizing life, such as lentils and hard-boiled eggs. Meat and wine are not consumed during Shiva because these symbolize joy.

The meal is a private matter, though. Only close family members participate. The meal is followed by the "Grace after meals," which is a religious prayer.

HINDU TRADITIONS

Because Hindus believe in reincarnation, funerals can be a celebration as much as a remembrance. In contrast to the Jewish funeral, mourners usually wear white and traditional Indian clothing. It may be best to call to avoid wearing anything that may offend.

THE ETIQUETTE INVOLVED

Also, in stark contrast to the Jewish tradition, flowers and sweetmeats are passed around. Expect noise. Do not be surprised to hear bells and horns.

If your friend is the eldest son or a male in the family, he traditionally represents the family in saying farewell to the deceased. He may shave his head as a sign of respect. In fact, many of the males may do the same.

"What the caterpillar perceives is the end, to the butterfly is just the beginning."

He may also be responsible for the cremation. This may be difficult for non-Hindus. But remember, he is showing respect for the one who has passed. The belief is that cremation releases the spirit from the body.

After the ceremony, the family will meet for a meal and prayers to begin a thirteen-day mourning period. Friends may visit to offer condolences during this time.

BUDDHIST TRADITIONS

Life is a journey.
Death is a return to the earth.
The universe is like an inn.
The passing years are like dust.

Regard this phantom world
As a star at dawn,
A bubble in a stream,
A flash of lightning in a summer cloud,
A flickering lamp -
A phantom - and a dream.

Vairacchedika 32 (Diamond Sutra)

The Buddhist religion is varied. In fact, there are more than 500 variations of Buddhism. Most believe in reincarnation. Accordingly, they typically cremate their loved ones.

However, there is no *one* tradition to follow for burial services or grieving. You may need to contact a family member to find out exactly how you should dress and if there will be a gathering after the funeral.

Most commonly, the service is simple and held in the crematorium with Buddhist readings. The emphasis is placed on the state of mind of the departed before he passed.

ISLAMIC TRADITIONS

Since burial must be within 24 hours of death, as a friend, it may not be possible to offer much comfort.

THE ETIQUETTE INVOLVED

It is helpful to remember that in the Islamic religion, death is a blessing, as it is believed that the departed is returning to his God. However, if you are a close friend and the same gender as the departed, you may attend the burial. Men attend a man's burial and women attend a woman's funeral. The gathering directly after the burial is for family only.

Traditionally, mourners should not cook for him or herself for forty days, so you may wish to provide a meal for your grieving friend. She will stay in the house of the departed for a period, so you will have to visit her. The length of time depends on the family's personal beliefs. Contacting your friend is the best way to discover exactly how you may help.

CHRISTIAN TRADITIONS

Christians tend to be all over the religious fervor map and have varied feelings about death.

While black remains the traditional color of mourning, it's not uncommon to see attendees dressed in bright hues. Some mourners even adopt a jovial demeanor, choosing to celebrate life and its ongoing journey. Still, the most familiar scene is one of somber faces and hushed tones.

THE ETIQUETTE INVOLVED

Traditionally, there may be a religious ceremony during the funeral. This depends, of course, on the family. You may experience a long Catholic Mass or a special service that includes a eulogy by a family member or close friend. Often, prayers are offered at the gravesite or after the casket is removed if it is a cremation.

Most Christian funerals are followed by a gathering at either a church or the family of the deceased's home. Friends and family gather, sharing food and stories concerning the one who has passed.

If attending, it is best to put aside your ideas of how others should display grief. As an etiquette consultant, I receive many emails from those disappointed about fellow mourners at funerals and wakes. Most commonly, the complainant feels that there isn't enough *quiet* decorum. *Be observant & follow along.*

There is no right or wrong way to grieve, and we shouldn't judge. We should consider the person who has passed and consider those who are grieving.

Everyone is different. So, say you are comforting a grieving friend. Say that your friend's deceased husband was a member of a motorcycle club. More than likely, you will find several leather-clad mourners. This is appropriate because the people who attend a funeral are doing so as a display of respect for the one who has passed, and to support those who are left to grieve.

More on this in the "Funerals in General" section.

NATIVE AMERICANS

In the early 1700s, the Iroquois buried their loved ones in a grave lined with skins along with useful, everyday items.

The Huron male next of kin would resurrect the deceased by adopting the man's children. They believed everyone would be resurrected in the end.

In the past, many Native Americans buried their dead above ground using trees or canoes. Most tribes held their own unique ceremonies to honor those who had passed.

WHAT TO EXPECT TODAY

Today, due to cultural blending and the diversity of tribes, funeral and mourning ceremonies differ widely.

The funeral may be traditional with traditional Native American clothing, including beautiful feathers. Traditional music might be performed along with dancing. In contrast, you might encounter a typical Christian-style funeral atmosphere with black clothing and somber demeanor. Again, as a friend, know who you are honoring and supporting.

FUNERALS IN GENERAL

There is no one etiquette rule for attending a funeral.

Here in the United States, we are fortunate to be enriched with our many different cultures and religions. To expect one set of etiquette rules for funerals or grieving is impractical or simply impossible. Everyone is different.

If I believe that my grandmother is going to a better place after she dies, most likely, I would feel comfortable celebrating her passing with a wake after the funeral. If anyone wants to cry, fine. If someone wants to sing, fine. It is an individual choice how we grieve and bury our beloved.

Recently, I found a newspaper article supporting my thesis. A woman, attending a funeral, was appalled at the hugging, the attire, and the behavior of attendees (it was a Christian funeral). She believed that a funeral is a somber, formal affair.

As I mentioned in my book, *From Casual to Formal: Your Wardrobe Decoder*, there is no *one* reality because everyone has their own perceptions of reality. This was a good example. Many people responded to this article with *their* stories of sharing love and not caring or even remembering the clothing of the attendees.

ETIQUETTE TO CONSIDER

Funerals are about saying goodbye, connecting with those who love you, and respecting the recently passed in the *fashion in which they lived*. Show respect through your attire and actions.

Always consider who the deceased person was and those who are left behind to grieve.

Please send condolences as soon as possible, as the grieving loved ones tend to feel alone, confused, and overwhelmed at this time. Don't worry about mentioning the deceased; many people feel the need to talk about their loved one. And please stay in touch.

The grieving process may take some time. Often, after a month, most support fades away. The final emotional impact of loss often surfaces gradually. Your friend might need the most support not immediately, but between one month and a year later, as the reality settles in.

If you experience the passing of a loved one, a thank-you note is expected within a month to all who sent flowers or assisted in any manner. However, if you are in this position, most won't fault you if you forget.

In addition, please talk to someone, anyone, and everyone. Talking about your loss will help you with your grief. It may not seem so, but trust me, in time it will.

My adult daughter died of brain cancer. This horrible disease took her in only ten months. Although she died two years ago, my mind wanders to that day in the hospital, watching her struggle for her last breath. Grieving takes time.

If you are grieving, you have my sincerest condolences.

BIRTHDAYS

HISTORICAL PERSPECTIVE

The first birthday party was not a party at all, but an attempt to ward off evil spirits. During this time, many believed that spirits would visit people on their birthdays. Family and friends would visit with the birthday person, sharing good wishes and thoughts. People gradually embraced the idea that giving gifts brought joy and helped ward off evil.

Historically, birthday celebrations were reserved for royalty and nobility in early European societies. Over time, Germany began honoring children's birthdays, marking a shift toward more inclusive traditions. Today, nearly every country and culture has developed its own way of celebrating a child's special day.

BIRTHDAY CUSTOMS

In Ireland, a child is held upside down and "bumped" on the floor—one bump for each year. The Japanese birthday child wears all new clothes, and on some birthdays, he visits a shrine. And in Nepal, the child receives a mixture of rice, yogurt, and color to mark his forehead for luck.

CHOICES AND ETIQUETTE

Thus, as you can see, there are many ways to celebrate birthdays. Luckily, we have the choice to decide what we prefer, regardless of traditional customs. If we decide to celebrate, it is our decision.

Even so, if we decide to invite guests to our birthday celebration, we should not pressure guests into buying a present just because we want to celebrate our special day. This is also true for inviting guests to a family member's birthday party. The best gift is free: thoughtfulness. This is what guests give when they share our day.

BIRTHDAY PARTY QUESTION

Question:

Is it proper to list on a birthday invitation: In lieu of a gift, please add to his college fund?

Birthday Invites

Reply:

Dear Birthday Invites,

Sorry, but no. All gifts are optional, even though most expect gifts for the birthday child. One option would be to mention your preference to a friend or family member who will spread the word. However, it is not polite to expect gifts, especially to suggest what those gifts should be.

Sincerely,

Rebecca

COMING OF AGE CELEBRATIONS

Quinceañera in the San Francisco de Asís church in Valle de
Bravo, Mexico

SPECIAL BIRTHDAYS

Still, some birthdays are even more special. This is especially true with "Coming of Age" birthdays.

These birthdays are usually traditional symbols of adulthood. Some have religious significance. Here, we explore some of the most followed customs.

THE QUINCEAÑERA

Quinceañeras del bicentenario

In Mexico and numerous Hispanic cultures globally, turning fifteen signifies a girl's coming of age, traditionally marked by a ceremony that presents her to the community as a young woman. This is an elaborate reconfirmation to the church (mass) paired with a ceremony called a Quinceañera.

The celebration is extravagant, with the teens dressed formally. After she is introduced as a woman at mass, the family and friends celebrate with a dance (the Quinceañera) in her honor. During the celebration, the father dances with his daughter, and others then join in. Gifts are usually substantial, including money.

Those in and along the Equator celebrate this event slightly differently. The 15-year-old girl, dressed in a pink dress, is accompanied by 14 girls and 14 boys, all formally dressed. Before the dance, the father slips the young lady's first pair of high heels on her feet. They dance the waltz, and her friends join in.

BAR MITZVAH & BAT MITZVAH

Two of the most recognizable examples of coming-of-age celebrations are the Bar Mitzvah, for boys, and the Bat Mitzvah for girls. These Jewish coming-of-age ceremonies are celebrated after their thirteenth birthday.

These begin with a religious ceremony followed by a reception at the synagogue. It typically includes a party later for the invited few. Usually a formal affair, those invited to this private party are expected to bring a gift—money is appropriate.

First Communion & Confirmation

First Communion, for children six or seven years old, and Confirmation, for eleven to fifteen years old, are ceremonies to confirm and reconfirm faith.

Confirmation is extremely significant to those who follow this faith, as the child is formally introduced to the community as a member of the church. Both celebrations are formal and are followed by receptions at the church. There are also invitation-only parties at home. Gifts of religious symbols or money are expected.

SWEET 16 & DEBUTANTES

When tracing historical facts, it appears that Sweet 16 parties – and the celebration of a girl turning 16 – began in 17th-century England to announce a young lady as *available* to prominent men of the Royal Court.

This is very similar to the idea of becoming a debutante. Very wealthy families began this tradition to announce and introduce the young lady to prospective wealthy young men, with marriage as the intended result.

Today, the typical sweet sixteen birthday is all about fun. In truth, it *is* a party to celebrate coming out as an adult or at least a teen with more options. Nevertheless, for the most part, it's all about celebrating a significant year.

A debutant ball, on the other hand, is very formal. The young ladies can often be older, even twenty-one years old. Although it isn't as common these days, when it is held, this event is usually hosted for a group of debutantes. These ladies are typically "sponsored" or have been chosen by a specific group. Most often, a charity group hosts this ball.

A debutante's attire is typically a very formal, long white dress with a full skirt. White gloves and pearls are the perfect accessories. Their escorts wear tuxedos.

Debutantes are expected to display superior social skills, including a curtsy, proper posture, and flawless conversational skills.

The event begins with an introduction of each debutante, followed by a formal meal and ball. It is advisable to take ballroom dancing and table manners classes beforehand.

GRADUATION

SIGNIFICANCE AND OBLIGATIONS

Graduation, whether from high school or college, is a special coming-of-age event. Considerable work has gone into this *one* accomplishment, marking this day deserving of a celebration.

However, the graduate has some responsibilities. For example, graduates must attend all graduation practices and should invite guests early. Usually, the school provides the graduate with a timeline and instructions for all these tasks.

ATTIRE CHOICES

On graduation day, make careful attire choices. Many times, the school offers suggestions. If not, consider the color of your gown. If it is white or a lighter color, choose light-colored clothes.

Often, young men are asked to wear a tie. This is simply a nod to tradition and to the event's reverence. In any case, consider more formal attire to represent the significance of the day. Remember, you will have to live with all the pictures taken of you that day. Choose carefully.

Tempting as it may be to skip under-gown attire for laughs, many who do end up regretting that choice. Trust me—there will be plenty of time to celebrate later. For now, keep it classy and avoid anything that might embarrass you or your loved ones.

Alternatively, your shoes may be the only visible article of attire seen due to the gown. Therefore, pay special attention to your shoe choice.

INVITATIONS AND ANNOUNCEMENTS

Only send invitations to close family, as there are scant few offered to you. Choose carefully. Unfortunately, some may view announcements as a plea for gifts. So, only send invitations to very close family. It may be helpful to mention that you are not interested in gifts to those who can help spread the word.

GRADUATION PARTY & GIFTS

A graduation is an event to celebrate the graduate's accomplishments. So, we party. Invite close friends, acquaintances, and special guests, such as godparents, to your party. It may be best to keep this small and not to expect gifts.

Although graduates might invite others from their graduating class, it may not be the best idea. It may become too exhausting for everyone to attend so many parties.

Parents often ask me about gift expectations for every party. No, we only give to those near and dear to our hearts, such as family and children of close friends.

With gifts received during the party, we don't open them in front of guests unless the guest requests it. In this case, you would open it out of sight of other guests. Write thank-you notes promptly.

A question often asked is what constitutes a good graduation gift. As in all things, it depends on the person. If the graduate is continuing their education, something they will need for this transition might be a great choice. This could be a gift certificate, luggage for their trip, or even cash for incidentals ($50+). If the person isn't continuing or just delaying their education journey, perhaps a useful gift they can enjoy, such as an electronic item, is best.

GRADUATION PARTY QUESTIONS

Question:

Hello from New Jersey,

My wife and I received an invitation from one of my friends to attend his wife's college graduation party at a VFW hall. They are adults in their forties.

The invitation clearly states at the bottom, "Please, no presents, just your presence." Is it proper etiquette to honor that request? Would giving a gift, such as money or a gift certificate, be inappropriate or potentially embarrassing? I truly want to respect my friend's wishes, but I also don't want to come across as stingy or thoughtless.

Thanks,

Visitors from New Jersey

Reply:

Dear New Jersey,

Hello from California!

When an invitation states, "no gifts," that is exactly what is expected. However, if you wish to give, you could give a gift certificate to a restaurant or bookstore (or something similar) to place into her card. That is usually a welcome gift and not ostentatious.

Sincerely,

Rebecca

Question:

I have a wonderful problem, but I can't decide the correct way to handle it, even after asking several friends. We have four children. Our three oldest are graduating from various schools this coming May. Our oldest daughter is graduating from law school (Stetson); our next daughter is graduating from college (FSU), and our youngest daughter is graduating from high school. In the past, I've given my daughters a party for their graduation. However, this May, I'm not sure what to do.

I would love to give one big party to celebrate them all together. They also like the idea. However, I hesitate to put my friends in a position of giving three gifts for one party. In addition, I'm not sure if it would be appropriate to "expect" gifts for our oldest daughter, who is graduating from law school. I hope that she will soon be employed and making a good income. Nevertheless, the younger two girls are expecting nice gifts (usually money) to help with their next path in life.

What is your opinion on this? Should I combine their parties and somehow specify NOT to gift the one daughter, but not mention the other two? That seems weird. No one knows the "protocol" for this situation.

I anxiously await your reply.

Visitor

Reply:

Dear Visitor,

Congratulations on your three daughters' accomplishments. That is incredible.

There is no correct answer or protocol for this question. However, this is my opinion.

While gift-giving is always optional, most people want to reward graduates. A single large party won't give each young lady the individual spotlight she's earned. To alleviate the issue of guests buying multiple gifts, the parties can be spread out over time, even though all the ladies graduate in May. Guests can then decide on gifts for each celebration.

Sincerely,

Rebecca

ANNIVERSARIES

How We Celebrate These Special Dates

Anniversaries are milestones and special dates that deserve a celebration. As in all things, however, we should consider the people we are celebrating and their preferences if we are guests or hosts of others' parties.

All anniversaries are different. In a couple's early years, they typically host their own parties. Gifts are optional because it seems rude to *ask* for presents and to create a gift-giving event for oneself. Consequently, sharing in the couple's joy of being together is the focus of these parties—or should be. Considering today's divorce rate, *any* anniversary is a joy to share.

Often, however, the couple celebrates these anniversaries alone, creating romantic interludes for just the two of them.

BENCHMARK ANNIVERSARIES

As the couple celebrates anniversaries together – and in deference to the early years – the couple's children, a family member, or close friend, may host anniversary parties for the latter years (20th>).

It's always a kind gesture to bring a gift to a wedding anniversary, even if it isn't strictly required. Still, the challenge is that the couple often already has a house full of items. So, how do you find the right gift? The secret, as always, is to choose something based on your personal knowledge of the couple.

Often, knowing the couple has always wanted to travel or own a particular item, the host will ask for contributions toward that goal. The host typically purchases the item, and everyone who contributes signs a congratulatory card. Of course, this must be done carefully, and donations should be optional. Guests may also contribute to the couple's favorite cause.

ANNIVERSARY QUESTION

Question:

Dear Rebecca,

My sister passed away last year. This is my brother-in-law's first year without her for what would have been their 40th anniversary. I want to let him know that he is still family, even though she is gone, and acknowledge the anniversary somehow. Would a card be appropriate?

Visitor

Reply:

Dear Visitor,

Please accept my sincere condolences for your loss.

A letter might be the best way to convey your feelings, as a card is a bit too generic. Write about your memories of times that all of you spent together, while stating that all of you are forever family. This might help him through this difficult milestone date.

Sincerely,

Rebecca

RETIREMENT

RETIREMENT PARTY ETIQUETTE

Retirement parties are as different as those who are retiring. As I have stated earlier, we need to remember for whom we are celebrating.

Tailor the party to the person's taste and the job the retiree is leaving. Keep in mind that not everyone enjoys attention or jokes about age, as some may find it uncomfortable rather than endearing. So be mindful and consider these sensitivities carefully when organizing the event.

A close friend, who was extremely unhappy at her job, retired recently. Therefore, even though she had worked for the same company for over twenty years, there was no reference to work at her party. The focus was on the future and her newly acquired free time.

Gifts are optional, but close family and friends may want to give the newly retired a gift related to a hobby or an interest. Restaurant or bookstore gift certificates are typically a good choice also. Still, it is typically not a gift-giving event.

CHRISTMAS

WHY FOCUS ON CHRISTMAS?

First, I want to apologize for only mentioning one religious holiday and ignoring others. However, this particular holiday deserves a little attention, and a reality check.

I could mention several religious holidays in this book, as each has its own unique etiquette and customs. However, it really isn't necessary. Everyone has a particular way to celebrate, which is as it should be. It will become clearer why I've singled out Christmas in the following pages.

A LITTLE HISTORY LESSON

I could drone on about the number of holidays we have and the crass commercialism of it all. For now, I will just say a few words about Christmas beginning with a little history.

In the 4th century, the Catholic Church mandated December 24th the celebration date of Christ's birth, to compete with the Roman birthday of the Sun God, Mithras. Although historians believe Jesus' birthday was in the spring.

In those days, people did not celebrate birthdays, and it was slow to catch on. Nevertheless, the church feared the pagan popularity and made the celebration compulsory.

SANTA?

In truth, there was a real Santa Claus, and he loved children. St. Nicholas was born in Turkey in the 4th century. He was religious, devoted, and generous. The Romans captured, tortured, and then imprisoned him.

Upon Constantine's accession, Saint Nicholas was freed and subsequently served as a delegate to the council. It was in this role that he performed his notable acts of charity. Ultimately, Saint Nicholas was designated the patron saint of children and sailors.

In the 6th century, the Dutch kept the legend alive—though they embellished it a bit. Children began placing their wooden shoes outside, hoping to find them filled with gifts by morning.

In time, St. Nicholas became Sinterklaas and finally the Anglican Santa Claus. It wasn't until 1823 and Clement C. Moore's story "The Night before Christmas" that our traditional jolly man in the red suit became popular.

WHAT DOES IT ALL MEAN?

Where am I going with this look back in history? Consider where the tradition began and what it is supposed to represent. We create our own family traditions. Considering Christmas, should children think of this day as the day they get *everything* they want?

It is only human nature to want to give to our loved ones. Even so, consider applying the brakes—just a bit. When we place too much importance on dollar amounts, on just this one day, we could be causing excessive pressure and stress on everyone involved.

It seems insurmountable that any of us could live up to such high expectations. We are not treating ourselves or our loved ones with kindness or respect when *things* are the focus.

GIFT-GIVING QUESTION

Question:

I feel deeply hurt by my brother's lack of fairness. We give gifts to his children, but he gives gifts to other family members' children, but not mine. We have never had issues between us before. So, I don't know how to deal with this. My children notice, which is the worst part. What is your advice on how to deal with poor behavior??

Giftless in Seattle

Reply:

Dear Giftless in Seattle,

Even though all gift-giving is optional, on the surface, this appears hurtful and deliberate. I would suggest asking him whether he would rather skip the gift exchange. You would then decide to continue at that point. If he is truly giving to others' children and not yours, he may have his reasons. There is no way to know exactly why without asking. As inconsiderate and disappointing as this is for your children, perhaps you could use this as a teachable moment and be very honest with your children about the fact that some people do not buy gifts. Sometimes they may feel pressured to buy for some but skip those they feel won't care (as sis, you'll still love him--no pressure).

Sincerely,

Rebecca

TRADITIONS TO SHARE

TRADITIONS IN THE U.S.

I would like to include a few words about the wonderful traditions we have in the United States. We live in a diverse country with rich and varied cultures. These cultures arrive with a trunk filled with interesting customs and traditions.

Look around and decide for yourself which customs and traditions you want to incorporate into your life. I personally love the Asian tradition of taking shoes off before entering a home.

In addition, we began a birthday tradition of our own. We celebrate each other's birthdays by spending time together over a meal—the birthday baby chooses the menu.

Choose or create customs and traditions for yourself and enjoy your loved ones.

PHOTOGRAPH CREDIT

Cover and Page 3: (3 photos) Pregnant Woman in Outdoor Setting; Guardian angel statue in graveyard; Newlywed couple standing with their parents; Copyright 2010 Ron Chapple Stock; © Royalty-Free/Corbis. Photos included with the Serif WebPlus program; Designed with Serif DrawPlus

Cover and Page 3: Old Jerusalem, Jewish boy reads Bar Mitzvah at the Western Wall, Jewish boy reads Bar Mitzvah.JPG

https://commons.wikimedia.org/wiki/File:Jewish_boy_reads_Bar _Mitzvah.JPG

Author: Peter van der Sluijs

License: Creative Commons Attribution-Share Alike 3.0 Unported, 2.5 Generic, 2.0 Generic, and 1.0 Generic licenses.

Alterations: Designed with Serif DrawPlus; Adjusted size to fit on the page

Cover and Page 3: Girl at her quinceañera in the San Francisco de Asís church in Valle de Bravo, Mexico; QuinceañeraSanFranValleBravo.JPG;

https://commons.wikimedia.org/wiki/File:QuinceañeraSanFranV alleBravo.JPG

Author: AlejandroLinaresGarcia

License: Creative Commons Attribution-Share Alike 4.0 International, 3.0 Unported, 2.5 Generic, 2.0 Generic, and 1.0 Generic license.

Alterations: Designed with Serif DrawPlus; Adjusted size to fit on the page

Page 13 Wedding: Side profile of a newlywed couple holding hands on a lawn; Copyright 2010 Ron Chapple Stock; © Royalty-Free/Corbis; Photo included with the Serif WebPlus program; Designed with Serif DrawPlus program

Page 21 Wedding Showers: Christmas gift. Copyright 2010 Ron Chapple Stock; © Royalty-Free/Corbis. Photo included with the Serif WebPlus program; Designed with the Serif DrawPlus program

Page 27 Baby Shower: Pregnant Woman in Outdoor Setting; Page: Baby shower page: Pregnant Woman in Outdoor Setting; Copyright 2010 Ron Chapple Stock; © Royalty-Free/Corbis. Photo included with the Serif WebPlus program; Designed with the Serif DrawPlus program

Page 31 Funerals & Grieving: Guardian angel statue in graveyard. Copyright 2010 Ron Chapple Stock; © Royalty-Free/Corbis. Photo included with the Serif WebPlus program; Designed with the Serif DrawPlus program

Page 45 Birthdays: Wrapped gifts; Copyright 2010 Ron Chapple Stock; © Royalty-Free/Corbis. Photo included with the Serif WebPlus program; Designed with the Serif DrawPlus program

Page 49 Coming of Age Celebrations: Girl at her quinceañera in the San Francisco de Asís church in Valle de Bravo, Mexico;

QuinceañeraSanFranValleBravo.JPG;

https://commons.wikimedia.org/wiki/QuinceañeraSanFranValleBravo.JPG

Author: AlejandroLinaresGarcia

License: Creative Commons Attribution-Share Alike 4.0 International, 3.0 Unported, 2.5 Generic, 2.0 Generic and 1.0 Generic license.

Alterations: Designed with Serif DrawPlus; Adjusted size to fit on page

Page 51 The Quinceañera: Quinceañeras del bicentenario (4528325145).jpg;

https://commons.wikimedia.org/wiki/File:Quinceañeras_del_bicentenario_(4528325145).jpg

Author: Eneas De Troya from Mexico City, México

License: Creative Commons Attribution 2.0 Generic license.

Alterations: Designed with Serif DrawPlus; Adjusted size to fit on page

Page 53 Bar Mitzvah & Bat Mitzvah: Old Jerusalem, Jewish boy reads Bar Mitzvah at the Western Wall; Jewish boy reads Bar Mitzvah.JPG

https://commons.wikimedia.org/wiki/File:Jewish_boy_reads_Bar_Mitzvah.JPG

Author: Peter van der Sluijs

License: Creative Commons Attribution-Share Alike 3.0 Unported, 2.5 Generic, 2.0 Generic, and 1.0 Generic licenses.

Alterations: Adjusted size to fit on page

Page 55 Debutante Ball: 58th International Debutante Ball 2012, New York City (Waldorf-Astoria Hotel); 58th International Debutante Ball 2012, New York City (Waldorf-Astoria Hotel).jpg https://commons.wikimedia.org/wiki/File:58th_International_De butante_Ball_2012,_New_York_City_(Waldorf-Astoria_Hotel).jpg
Author: Antondbe
License: Creative Commons Attribution-Share Alike 4.0 International license.
Alterations: Designed with Serif DrawPlus; Adjusted size to fit on the page

Page 57 Graduation: Photo included with the Serif WebPlus program; Designed with the Serif DrawPlus program; Author unknown

Page 65 Anniversaries: Man Giving Gift to Woman at Restaurant; Copyright 2010 Ron Chapple Stock; © Royalty-Free/Corbis. Photo included with the Serif WebPlus program

Page 68 Retirement: Designed with Serif DrawPlus

Page 71 Christmas: Christmas presents under the tree; Copyright 2010 Ron Chapple Stock; © Royalty-Free/Corbis. Photo included with the Serif WebPlus program

Page 77 Traditions to Share: Photo included with the Serif WebPlus program; Author unknown

Methodology of Crediting Photographs Used

To give credit to each photographer, I followed the directions provided by Creative Commons and per the wishes of each author.

YOUR AUTHOR

Your author, Rebecca Black, also known as The Polite One, retired from her company, **Etiquette Now!,** after a successful and rewarding 20+ years. As the owner and facilitator of her company, this retired elementary school teacher designed and presented custom etiquette workshops for individuals, corporate, governmental, and educational clients. Due to her extensive knowledge of the subject, she is also a well-respected author of etiquette books and lesson plans.

Considered an expert in the field, Rebecca provides etiquette Q&A and advice through her blogs: Got Etiquette Advice, Got Wedding Etiquette, and The Polite One's Insights.

Although Rebecca focused her writing on etiquette issues for decades, she is currently following her passion for writing fiction. A few of her most recent children's books also focus on the environment: *Save the Jellywonkers: Help Keep The Oceans Clean; Beware the Blackness, A Jellywonker Adventure;* and *The Tale of a Bear & Pony: A Yellowstone Adventure.* Her anti-bullying book, *He Took My Sister, A Joy Bell Mystery*, is an effort to help those plagued by bullies.

For junior teens and young adults, the newly rewritten tenth anniversary edition of the Sapphire Series Trilogy emphasizes the theme of love versus greed, featuring a young girl who becomes a hero.

And please check out her newly published *Evolution of the Cyborg,* a tale of the arrogance and greed of one who will do anything to gain from the fragility of the human body.

Please visit rebeccablackauthor.blogspot.com for more information about Rebecca's current news.

Connect with Us

https://www.facebook.com/ThePoliteOne

https://www.facebook.com/rebeccablackauthor/

Visit Us

Author Rebecca Black

Etiquette Now! Insights

Got Etiquette Advice

Got Wedding Etiquette

Living Well Etc.

The Polite One's Insights

The Polite Traveler

https://www.amazon.com/author/rebecca_black

Published Fiction Books by Rebecca Black

The Tale of a Bear & Pony; A Yellowstone Adventure

Save The Jellywonkers! -- Help Keep Our Oceans Clean

Beware the Blackness! A Jellywonker Adventure

Sapphire and the Atlantians; War in Atlantis; The Return of the Tui Suri

He Took My Sister: A Joy Bell Mystery

Evolution of The Cyborg

Published Etiquette Books by Rebecca Black

Dining Etiquette: Essential Guide for Table Manners, Business Meals, Sushi, Wine and Tea Etiquette

Dress for All Occasions—The Basics, Attire Must-Haves, Dress Code Definitions & FAQs

Entertaining Skills 101: Lesson Plans for Those Who Wish to Present Workshops

Etiquette for the Important Events in Our Lives: Common sense etiquette with a side of history and a dollop of gift-giving savvy

Etiquette and Essential Life Skills for the Socially Savvy Adult: Feel Confident in All Situations

Etiquette and Essential Life Skills for the Socially Savvy Teen: Feel Confident in All Situations

Golf Etiquette: Civility on the Course

How to Eat Sushi Properly: A Beginner's Guide

How to Teach Your Children Manners: Essential Life Skills Your Child Needs to Know!

International Business Travel Etiquette: Seal the Deal by Understanding Proper Protocol

Organizational Skills for Teens: From Chaos to Clarity

Prom Etiquette: Designing Your Perfect Prom Experience

Reaching Your Potential: How to use our life lessons to grow as a person and to improve the workplace environment

Societal Rage: Problem-solving for our increasingly violent world

The Socially Savvy Sipper: From holding the glass to ordering a bottle of wine in a restaurant and everything in between

Tea O'Clock; A Delightful Guide to British Tea Times

Train the Trainer Guide: The essential guide for those who wish to present workshops and classes for adults

Wedding & Reception Planning: The Etiquette Guide for Planning the Perfect Wedding

Workplace Etiquette: How to Create a Civil Workplace

Published Lesson Plans

Business Meal Etiquette

Career Fair Etiquette

Entertaining Skills 101

Etiquette for the Socially Savvy Teen

Golf Etiquette

Growing Up Socially Savvy

How to Become a Socially Savvy Lady

How to Teach Your Children Manners

Just for Teens, Skills for the Socially Savvy

Manners for Children

Organizational Skills

Prom Etiquette

Proper Business Attire

Skills for the Socially Savvy and Well-Dressed Teen

Skills for the Socially Savvy and Well-Organized Teen

Table Manners

Tea O'Clock; A Delightful Guide to British Tea Times

Train the Trainer

Wine Etiquette

Workplace Etiquette

Wedding Lesson Plans

Lessons for the Newly Engaged

Wedding Planning

Wedding Reception Planning

Please visit https://www.amazon.com/author/rebecca_black for information about collecting more etiquette books.